Discover the Rich Heritage of the Philippines with

Bisaya Language
Flowers

Mark Satorre

Daisy
[dai-si]
Daisy

Gumamela
[gu-ma-me-la]
Hibiscus

Hydrangea
[hi-dran-je-ja]
Hydrangea

Anturyom
[an-tur-yom]
Anthurium

Bisaya Language: Flowers

Amapola
[a-mah-po-la]
Poppy Flower
Anturyom
[an-tur-yom]
Anthurium

Adelpa
[a-del-pah]
Oleander
Alissum
[a-lis-sum]
Sweet Alyssum

Baho–baho
[ba-ho-ba-ho]
Yellow–Vein Eranthemum
Bumbil
[boom-bil]
Bougainvillea

Balayong
[ba-lah-yung]
Palawan Cherry Blossom
Caballero
[ka-bal-ye-ro]
Fire Tree

Dalya
[dal-ya]
Dahlia
Daisy
[dai-si]
Daisy

Gladiolus
[gla-di-o-lus]
Gladiolus
Gumamela
[gu-ma-me-la]
Hibiscus

Heliconia
[he-li-ko-ni-ja]
Lobster Claw
Hydrangea
[hi-dran-je-ja]
Hydrangea

Hasinto
[ha-seen-tu]
Hyacinth
Ipil–ipil
[i-pil-i-pil]
Lead Tree

Ilang–ilang
[i-lang-i-lang]
Ylang–ylang
Impatiens
[im-pa-shens]
Busy Lizzie

Kadena de Amor
[ka-de-na de a-mor]
Coral Vine
Kandingkanding
[kan-ding-kan-ding]
Lantana

Kampanilya
[kam-pa-nil-ya]
Yellow Bell
Kulitis
[ku-li-tis]
Amaranth

Kalatsutsi
[ka-lat-sut-si]
Plumeria
Kumintang
[khu-min-tang]
Periwinkle

Kamia
[ka-mi-ja]
White Ginger Lily
Krisantemo
[kri-san-teh-mo]
Chrysanthemum

Lavender
[la-ven-dir]
Lavender
Liryo
[li-ryo]
Lily

Marabilya
[mah-ra-bil-ya]
Marigold
Mirasol
[mi-ra-sul]
Sunflower

Malabulak
[ma-la-bu-lak]
Red Silk–Cotton Tree
Narra
[na-ra]
Narra Tree

Orkid
[or-kid]
Orchid

Pagusi
[pah-goo-si]
Lotus

Palong
[pa-lung]
Cockscomb
Rafflesia
[ra-fles-i-a]
Corpse Flower

Rosas
[ro-sas]
Rose
Siar
[si-ar]
Yellow Flame Tree

Sampagita
[sam-pa-gí-ta]
Arabian Jasmine
Santan
[san-tan]
Jungle Geranium

Salingbobog
[sa-ling-bo-bog]
Sacred Garlic Pear Tree
Tayabak
[Tah-ya-bak]
Jade Vine

Tuberosa
[tu-be-ro-sa]
Tuberose
Tulip
[tu-lip]
Tulip